Together, We Can Do Anything

Written by Christina B. Grimes
Photography by Marah Mumma Photography

Photo credits: Marah Mumma Photography, Maria Vicencio Photography (page 11)

ISBN 978-0-692-25325-0

This book is inspired by my children Parker and Madison, who have shown me the most beautiful and patient sibling relationship.

When we first found out that our brother
had Down syndrome we didn't really know
what it meant,

but I have learned a lot from my sister
and now I love to tell people exactly what
it means to have a sibling with Down
syndrome.

It means having someone who will love me
unconditionally. My brother doesn't care what
wear, how I look, or whether I make a mistake
He supports me no matter what.

Kids with Down syndrome have an extra copy of the 21st chromosome inside each cell in their body. Inside these chromosomes are genes that give our bodies information that make us a girl or boy, short or tall, determine our eye color, and whether we have light or dark hair. Most people have 46 chromosomes in each cell, but people with Down syndrome have 47.

Kids who are born with Down syndrome will always have it, but it doesn't stop them from having all the same hopes and dreams about growing up.

Children with Down syndrome have all the
same emotions as other kids. Just like us,
our brother gets sad sometimes and needs a
friend to talk to, or a friend to celebrate with
when he is happy.

Everyone with Down syndrome is unique. Just like other children, they like to do different things. My sister and I like to play baseball together.

My sister loves to spend time with her friends and we like to go to concerts together.

Kids with Down syndrome may have similar physical traits like the shape of their eyes or nose, but everyone says my sister looks just like me.

Children with Down syndrome are born
into families of all skin colors.

Our brother has Down syndrome, but that isn't who he is. He is a kid just like us!

Many kids with Down syndrome have low muscle tone which may make it harder to walk or talk, but with a little extra time my brother still does everything I do.

My brother has therapists who come to our house and help him learn to use his muscles to play and speak. I like to help him practice too.

Sometimes our brother may need more time to understand things that he learns and he may need more practice with his teachers, but he goes to school just like us and works hard to learn.

Sometimes people have trouble
understanding what our brother says, but if
you take the time to ask him to say it again,
you will be glad you did.

Many people with Down syndrome
learn to use sign language to help them
communicate before they learn to speak.

My sister was born with a heart defect and the doctors worked hard to fix her heart, but sometimes she gets tired when we are playing. I don't mind taking a break with her and it doesn't take long before she is ready to play again.

With the love and support of family and friends, children with Down syndrome often grow up to be very successful adults who have jobs and give back to their community in many wonderful ways.

Our brother is an important part of our family
and we love him very much.

You see, my sister might have to work a little bit harder sometimes to do things that come easy to other kids, but she still enjoys doing all the same activities other kids do.

So now when people ask us what does it mean to have a sibling with Down syndrome? We smile and say…

having a sibling with Down syndrome
means having a best friend for life and
together we can do anything.

A couple was at the park swinging their baby on the swing. Samantha walks u[p] to them and says "Hi. My name is Sammie and your daughter is so cute. What [is] her name and how old is she?" The mom says "Her name is Emma and she is 2 months old." Sammie responds to her saying "Oh! Well this is my Lily and she [is] 18 months old. She has Down syndrome, but you know what, she's no differen[t] than anyone else. She's just the same like you and me, and I love her so much!" This made the mom smile and she looked at   Sammie's mom and said "You must be so proud." Samantha, age 7

"Mom, when I get married I want to adopt a child like Sammie with Down syndrome". Dalton, age 12

"My sister Sarah who has Down syndrome has changed my life. It benefits m[e] because I learn different things about people with disabilities. She also change[s] my perspective of those with Down syndrome." Trevor, age 13

"I think some of the benefits of having a sibling with Down syndrome include learning how to be a more compassionate or patient person, improving your teaching skills, becoming more loving, and to learn to accept everyone." Brian age 18

"I believe my sister Sammie made me the person that I am today. She has taug[ht] me to be more loving and patient and to have a better outlook on life." Andrea age 21

"Henry is very, very special. And we love him so much. He has Down syndrome. Down syndrome is an extra chromosome. And that means he is ver[y] very, very special. And Henry is so cute. He has a physical therapist named Mi[ss] Trudy. And some Tuesdays she comes over. Sometimes she comes with anothe[r] lady, Miss Staples. Down syndrome makes him very special. Addison goes to [a] special place with other children who have Down syndrome. The place is calle[d] FRIENDS. We love him so much with Down syndrome. We help Henry. Each of us kids get to do something. I get to help him sit up and learn to crawl. I ge[t] to help him stand so he can walk one day. This is my story about him. The End Elisabeth, age 6

"My brother has Down syndrome. That makes him special. It means he has an extra chromosome, but it doesn't hurt him. It just makes him extra special." Samuel, age 8

"Addi is so perfect. I love him." Aedan, age 10

"My brother likes to read and sing. He likes to play trains. We plan for him to go to Harvard. He likes to snuggle. He likes faces. Raspberries are his favorite form of communication." Nathaniel, age 11

"There are challenges, but everyone has a challenge. I have seen Addison overcome many things. No matter how hard it is he still keeps going. I believe that we received a precious gift when we were given Addison and I wouldn't want him any other way." Emma, age 14

"When I look at Henry I don't see Down syndrome. First, I see beautiful blue eyes that are always smiling and light up when anyone looks at him. Next, I see his smile, because if you smile at him, he will smile back. And what a smile! It melts my heart every time. Then I see a baby. When I see a baby, any baby, my first thought is "I wonder who they will be?" And when I look at little Addison it is not different. I believe he can do or be anything he wants." Brianna, age 18

"I'm of the conviction that Down syndrome is no accident, but that God created Henry just the way he is, as part of His plan for Henry's life. Until Henry knows what that is, we will help him to accomplish the vision God has given us: to change the face of Downs. To show the world that Downs isn't a curse, it's a challenge, the Christian's blessing in disguise. We each have a challenge. Some may struggle with their health. Some may have a speech impediment or a crippling fear of the future. But each of us has a challenge. Life isn't about being afraid of that challenge, but to overcome it. And with God's grace, we will." Kaitlin, age 22

My brother Noah has Down syndrome and he has taught me that just because you're different, doesn't mean you can't be AWESOME!" Halle, age 13

"Having a brother with Down syndrome has really affected my life in a positive way. I see through different eyes and hear through different ears. He has made me a better person and has opened my eyes to things that I would never have cared about if it weren't for him. I love you Noah, and I thank God for bringing us together." Sophie, age 20

"It was the year 1999; I was hardly 8 years old. I remember my dad telling me and my sister, between the tears, "He may be a little different but he is still your brother." So I looked at my brother, expecting him to be different, and couldn't see what my dad was talking about. Growing up, I never saw Noah as different. I saw my brother as a boy that likes to play in the dirt; a boy that loves to swim in the summer pools; a boy who hangs out with his friends; a boy that loves to learn and try new things; and finally, a boy who loves and forever gives love. Maybe it is selfish of me, but I wouldn't trade my brother for anyone else in the world. He has taught me to love, and accept, and cherish everyone and everything that enters my life. He has taught me to be a better person through his simplest of acts and ways of life. Today, if someone asks me, "Is your brother different?" I laugh. And I say "Yes, yes he is. And I wouldn't change it for the world." My brother isn't a little "different," he is special, and will always be my brother." Peyton, age 20

CPSIA information can be obtained
at www.ICGtesting.com
Printed in the USA
BVOW05*0911301017

498976BV00002B/2/P